I'm Reading About

NEVADA

The Silver State!

GALLOPADE

by Carole Marsh

Printed and Manufactured in Peachtree City, GA., USA
www.gallopade.com

Book design: John Hanson
Editorial manager: Janice Baker

Nevada is a great state.
It is one of a kind.

What makes Nevada special?
Let's read about it and see!

NATIVE AMERICANS

Who lived in Nevada first?

Native Americans did!

They moved around to find food.
They hunted for animals to eat.
They fished in Nevada's rivers.
They gathered fruits and seeds and nuts.

EXPLORERS

The first explorers came to Nevada in 1776.
They came from the country of Spain.

Francisco Garces was their leader.
He was a missionary.

SETTLEMENT

Mormon pioneers started the first settlement in Nevada. They named it Mormon Station. It was a trading post for people heading west.

Mormon Station later became known as Genoa, Nevada.

Genoa

STATEHOOD

Nevada was the 36th state
to join the United States of America!

Isn't it great,
to be a state!
I bet Nevada
could hardly wait!

Nevada became a state in 1864.

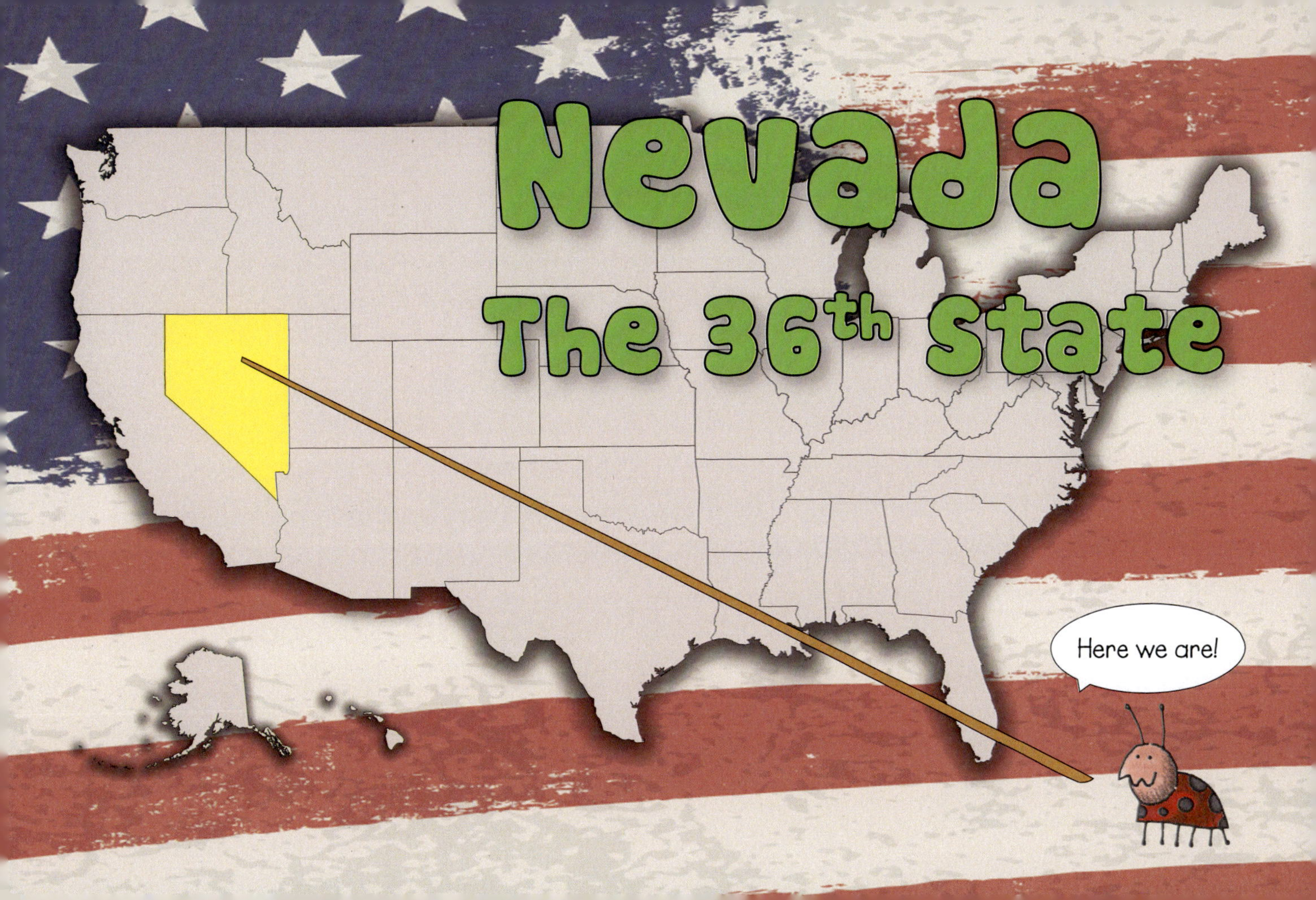
Nevada
The 36th State
Here we are!

FLAG

I am the state flag.
I was adopted in 1991.

What color am I?
I am blue.

Look at me.
What else do you see?

I fly high over the state of Nevada!

BATTLE BORN
NEVADA

CAPITAL

Say hello to Carson City,
the capital city of Nevada!

There is an important building in Carson City.
It is the State Capitol.
Nevada's laws are made there!

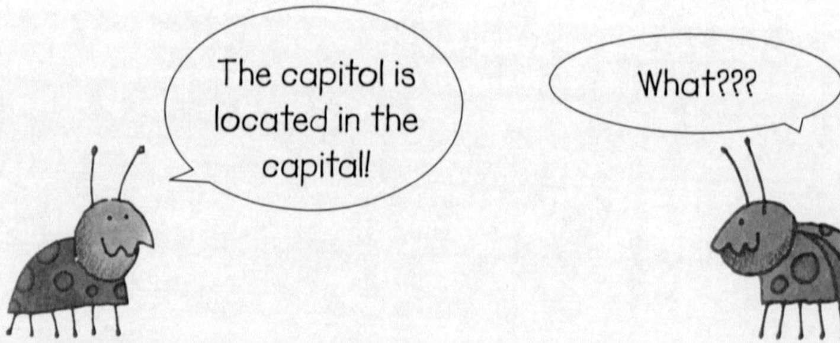

Capitol
Carson City
Capital

SEAL

I am a seal,
but I am not the State Seal.
If I were, I would be very important.
I would be stamped on many official papers.
(Ouch, that might hurt!)

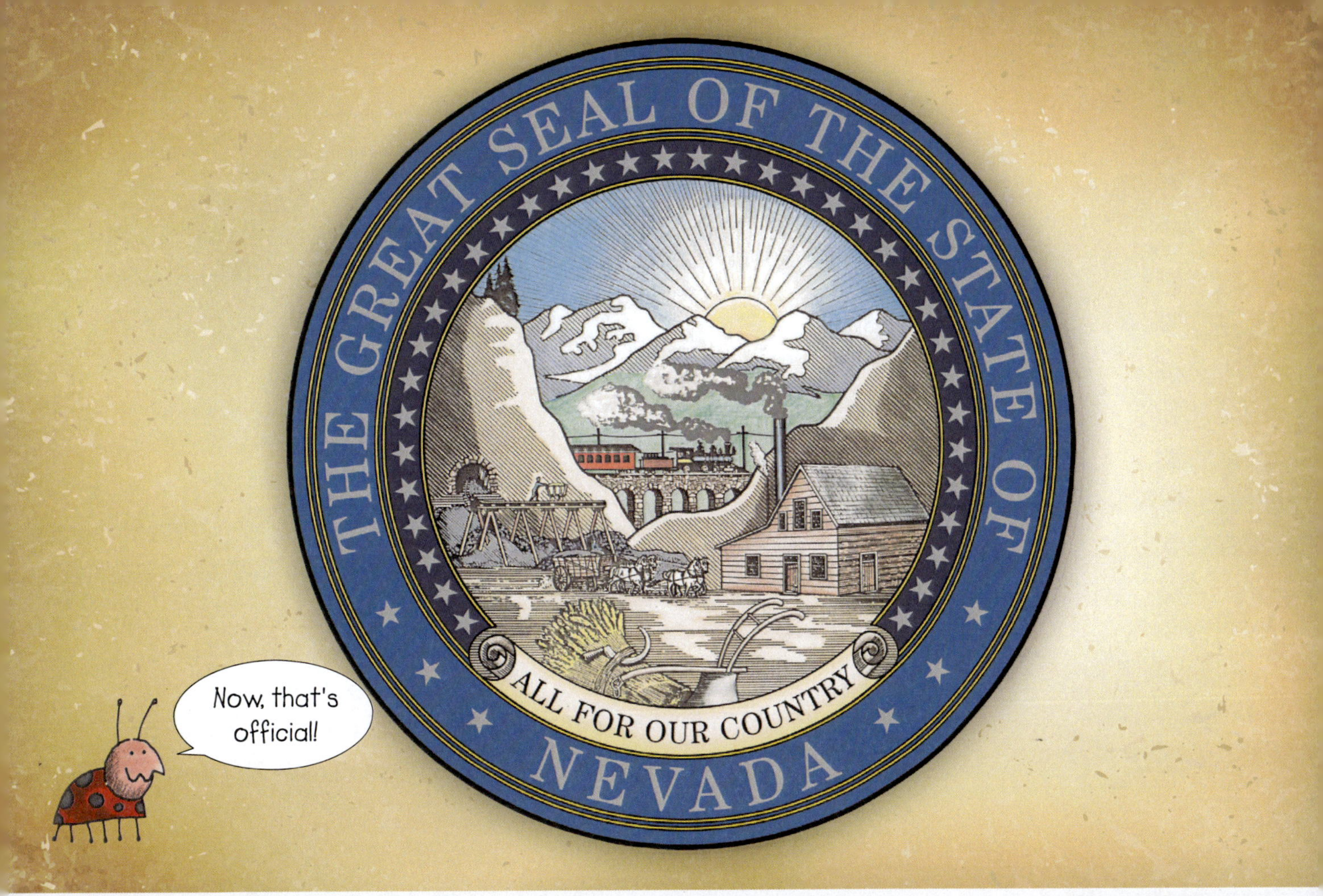
THE GREAT SEAL OF THE STATE OF
NEVADA
ALL FOR OUR COUNTRY
Now, that's official!

NICKNAME

State nicknames are fun!
State nicknames are great!
They share fun facts
about each state!

Nevada's nickname is "The Silver State."

Where did Nevada's nickname come from?
A lot of silver has been mined in Nevada!

The Silver State

BORDERS

Look at Nevada.
Nevada is in a region called "the Southwest."

Nevada borders five other states
Find them on the map!

Borders

OREGON
IDAHO
NEVADA
CALIFORNIA
UTAH
ARIZONA
Howdy, neighbors!

COUNTIES

Nevada is divided into 16 counties.
There is also one independent city in Nevada.
Counties are a form of local government.
Counties provide services that people need!

Those services include:

Schools **Libraries** **Firefighters**

Parks **Police** **and More!**

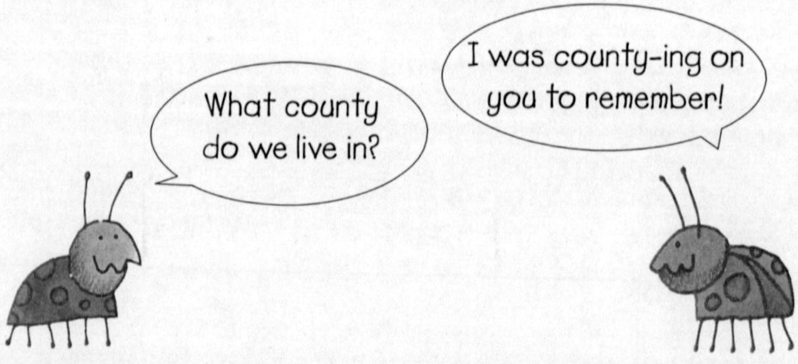

Counties

NEVADA'S CAPITAL,
CARSON CITY, WAS
NAMED AFTER
MOUNTAIN MAN
KIT CARSON.

Many famous people

Dat So La Lee

Native American artist known for basket weaving

Anne Martin

Helped women win the right to vote in Nevada

James E. Casey

Founder of United Parcel Service (UPS)

call our state home!

PEOPLE

Eva Bertrand Adams

Director of the U.S. Mint, where U.S. coins are made

Pat Nixon

First Lady and wife of President Richard Nixon

Andre Agassi

World champion tennis player

Mountain Bluebird

I am the state bird, and I fly
over Nevada, proud and high.

As I fly, up in the sky,
I flap my wings to tell you "Hi!"

The Nevada state bird is the Mountain Bluebird.

Sagebrush

FLOWER

I am Sagebrush.
I am the state flower.

I grow where it's warm and sunny.
My branches grow straight and tall.
I help make Nevada beautiful!

Look at me! Smell me!
I grow in the desert heat!

Single-Leaf Piñon

TREE

I am a Single-Leaf Piñon—I'm one of two state trees.
All over Nevada is where to find me.

My roots run deep, they keep me strong.
My leaves stay green, all year long.

I stand up straight, big and tall.
Don't climb too high—it would hurt to fall!

The Bristlecone Pine is
Nevada's other state tree.

Vivid Dancer Damselfly

I am the Vivid Dancer Damselfly.
I am the state insect.

My body is deep blue.
I flap my wings in the sunlight.

I live near springs and ponds.
Watch me fly over the water!

Desert

Let's go to the desert!

The desert is dry.
It hardly ever rains.

Temperatures are hot during the day,
but get cold at night!

Nevada's deserts are home to many animals:

Scorpions **Coyotes** **Snakes** **Tarantulas** **Hawks** **and More!**

DESERT

Sierra Nevada
Mountains

MOUNTAINS

Nevada's Sierra Nevada Mountains
are the place to be.
Hiking, fishing, camping—
fun for you and me.

Winter weather brings lots of snow.
Temperatures drop to freezing and below!

Rivers

RIVERS

Nevada has many rivers.
People like to use rivers
for boating and fishing!

This habitat is home to many animals:

Birds Deer Snakes Frogs Fish and More!

Carson City, Nevada's capital,
was built along the Carson River.

Hoover Dam

LANDMARK

The Hoover Dam is on the border of Nevada and Arizona!

The huge dam is built on the Colorado River. It keeps the river from flooding. It also provides power for Nevada, Arizona, and California.

The Hoover Dam is named after President Herbert Hoover!

Nevada Crops

AGRICULTURE

Nevada has many farms.
Why?
Because Nevada has good soil and a warm climate!

Some of the top crops grown in Nevada are:

Hay **Potatoes** **Wheat** **Barley**

Sports in Nevada

SPORTS

Baseball! Basketball! Football!
Nevada has it all.

Whether you like to watch or play,
You are sure to have a ball!

Rebels Wolf Pack & More!

Nevada: Home of the Las Vegas Strip

CLAIM TO FAME

Nevada is home to the Las Vegas Strip! Huge hotels and casinos line a four-mile road. Many of America's largest hotels are on the Las Vegas Strip.

All of the city lights make Las Vegas one of the brightest cities on Earth!

GLOSSARY

climate: weather conditions in an area over a long period of time

dam: a structure used to hold back water

habitat: a place where plants or animals naturally live

laws: rules made by the government

missionary: a person sent to an area to spread their religion

Mormon: a member of a religion started by Joseph Smith, Jr.

pioneer: a person who is the first to settle in a new area

region: an area that has similar characteristics

settlement: the first community in an area

trading post: a place to trade goods